COUPLE'S ADVENT CALENDAR

AN ESCAPE ROOM FOR TWO

WELCOME TO THE COUPLE'S ESCAPE ROOM

This year, your **Advent Calendar** won't be like the others: instead of chocolates, you'll find a series of challenges, puzzles, and special activities to do together.

Every day, starting from December 1st until Christmas Eve, you'll embark on a unique adventure, where you'll solve mysteries, complete missions, and build indelible memories as a couple.

This isn't just a simple Advent Calendar. It's a Christmas escape room, an opportunity to get into the true spirit of the holidays... but in an original and intriguing way!

Every activity you complete will bring you a little closer, making the days leading up to Christmas more fun, romantic, and full of surprises.

HERE'S WHAT AWAITS YOU...

Every day, a new puzzle or challenge: Every day, you will find a new activity to complete. It will be a true mini escape room, and the only way to move on to the next day is to solve the daily puzzle, challenge, or activity and mark it as completed. Your goal is to enjoy every step of the journey together, tackling fun and engaging puzzles that will test your connection and creativity.

Christmas Theme: Every puzzle and challenge will be inspired by the warm and festive atmosphere of Christmas. Decorations, lights, and the holiday spirit will accompany your path, setting the **perfect mood** for this special experience. Each day will be a new opportunity to immerse yourselves in the Christmas spirit with activities that will help you prepare for the most anticipated day of December.

A Journey for the Couple: This calendar is not just a game; it's an opportunity to experience an adventure together that will strengthen your bond and create unforgettable memories. Every day, by completing the challenge, you will get closer to a special Christmas filled with laughter, discoveries, and new moments to share.

BEFORE YOU START...

A FEW MORE THINGS TO KEEP IN MIND...

Mark Completed Activities: At the beginning of the activities, you will find a calendar where you can check off whether you have completed the puzzle or challenge.

No Crossover Clues: Each activity is self-contained, and there will be no clues that carry over between days. Every puzzle or game is designed to be conclusive on its own, so you can fully enjoy each day without confusion.

EXTRA TIPS

Timing the Game: Read the activities first thing in the morning to figure out the best time of day to complete them. Decide together how to organize your time, but always remember to mark the completed activities so you don't lose track of your adventure.

Rewards: After completing the day's activity, decide together on a small "reward" to celebrate, such as a special hug, a small loving gesture, or a piece of chocolate.

READY, SET, GO!

Let's dive into your personal couple's Christmas adventure!
Each step will bring you closer to Christmas with a dose of
fun, romance, and a touch of craziness!

Don't know what to expect? Well, that's the best part: every
day will be a surprise, but with one common goal... to have
fun, strengthen your bond, and create memories that will last
all year (and maybe even longer!).

ARE YOU READY?
THE COUNTDOWN HAS BEGUN... AND THE
ADVENTURE AWAITS AROUND EVERY CORNER!
🎄🎁

DAILY TRACKING

Pag. 1 ☐

Pag. 4 ☐

Pag. 7 ☐

Pag. 9 ☐

Pag. 11 ☐

Pag. 17 ☐

Pag. 18 ☐

Pag. 20 ☐

Pag. 23 ☐

Pag. 24 ☐

Pag. 28 ☐

Pag. 30 ☐

Pag. 31 ☐

Pag. 35 ☐

Pag. 36 ☐

Pag. 37 ☐

Pag. 38 ☐

Pag. 42 ☐

Pag. 43 ☐

Pag. 45 ☐

Pag. 48 ☐

Pag. 51 ☐

Pag. 53 ☐

Pag. 57 ☐

Solutions: Pag. 58

❤ 1

REFLECTION OF THE DAY
AS A COUPLE

Together, you will reconstruct a treasured memory piece by piece! As you put the pieces together, the final step will be to decipher the deeper gift—the significant message that the activity itself is trying to tell you.

WHAT TO DO DURING THE DAY

> PRINT A PHOTO OF YOURSELVES, OF A SPECIAL MOMENT, A TRIP, A UNIQUE MEMORY
> A4 OR LARGER FORMAT

> BUY CARDSTOCK THE SAME SIZE AS THE PRINTED PHOTO AND, IF YOU DON'T HAVE IT AT HOME, GLUE

IN THE EVENING... ARE YOU READY TO UNCOVER THE DAY'S MESSAGE

INSTRUCTIONS:

1. Get comfortable, turn on some relaxing lights, and put on a good playlist.
2. Cut the printed photo into pieces, larger or smaller, to increase the difficulty of the puzzle.

REVELATION. NOW, LOOK BEYOND THE IMAGE. WHAT DEEPER MEANING OR REFLECTION IS REVEALED THROUGH THE ACT OF REBUILDING THIS MOMENT TOGETHER? WRITE YOUR DISCOVERY BELOW.

SOME HINTS...

Hint 1 - **"Every piece matters"**

Hint 2 - **"An image, a special moment"**

Hint 3- **"It is given at Christmas to those you love"**

HAVE YOU COMPLETED THE PUZZLE?

Perfect...
Now it's time to write your answer below.

What is the essential meaning—the gift—hidden in this
shared activity?

FILL IN THE ANSWER TOGETHER

———————————————————————

———————————————————————

———————————————————————

The solution is provided in the last pages of the book (obviously, the result
is subjective; ours is a "solution" that points to the hidden significance).
Take a look and mark this first activity as complete.

DECORATION SCAVENGER HUNT

Find hidden objects to start warming up your holiday spirit.

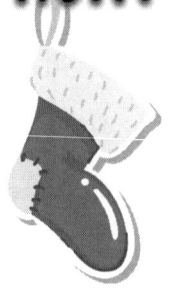

WHAT TO DO DURING THE DAY

IT'S TIME TO FIND THE CHRISTMAS DECORATIONS BOX...

FOUND IT? GREAT, TAKE 6 CHRISTMAS DECORATIONS... OF YOUR CHOICE.

EACH PERSON HIDES 3 OBJECTS AROUND THE HOUSE, AND WRITES NOTES WITH CLUES.

INSTRUCTIONS:

1. Each person **hides their 3 objects** around the house... hide them at the same time, so you make sure not to find the other person's objects while hiding your own.
2. **Write the clues** on a piece of paper to find the hidden objects. Here are some examples:

"A warm place where cookies rest" [the cupboard] "At the North Pole" [The freezer] "The porcelain throne room" [the bathroom]

Each time you find an object, call your partner to get the next note/clue.

REMEMBER... IT'S A COUPLE'S ESCAPE ROOM (SCAVENGER HUNT), SO IF YOUR PARTNER CAN'T FIND ALL THE OBJECTS, YOU MUST HELP THEM BY GIVING THEM MORE HINTS!

HAVE YOU FOUND ALL THE HIDDEN OBJECTS?

GREAT JOB, BUT IT'S NOT OVER YET...

Now for the most fun part: **decorate a section of the house with the objects you found!**

And snap a souvenir photo... you can print it and stick it below.

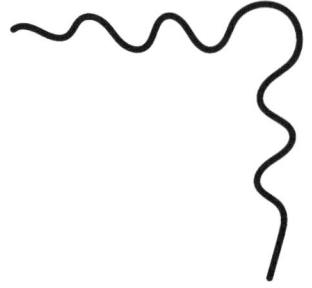

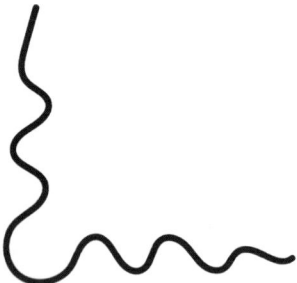

THE SECRET CHRISTMAS CODE

Decipher a secret Christmas code to
uncover a holiday message.

YOU ONLY NEED A PEN AND A LITTLE BIT OF TIME TO DECIPHER THE SECRET CODE

LETTER	NUMBER
A	1
B	2
C	3
D	4
E	5
F	6
G	7
H	8
I	9
J	10
K	11
L	12
M	13
N	14
O	15

LETTER	NUMBER
P	16
Q	17
R	18
S	19
T	20
U	21
V	22
W	23
X	24
Y	25
Z	26

9 14 - 20 8 5 - 3 15 12 4 - 15 6 - 23 9 14 20 5 18 - 20 8 5 - 23 1 18
13 20 8 - 15 6 - 20 8 5 - 12 9 7 8 20 19 - 18 5 13 9 14 4 19 - 21 19
- 20 8 1 20 - 3 8 18 9 19 20 13 1 19 - 9 19 - 1 12 23 1 25 19 - 3 12
15 19 5 18

♥ 4

CHRISTMAS SONGS

The Song (Christmas) Couple.

WHAT TO PREPARE DURING THE DAY

CREATE A SHARED SPOTIFY PLAYLIST OR WRITE DOWN CHRISTMAS SONGS ON YOUR PHONE

IF YOU CREATE A SHARED PLAYLIST, ADD CHRISTMAS SONGS YOU BOTH LIKE THROUGHOUT THE DAY...

THE KARAOKE NIGHT BEGINS

INSTRUCTIONS:

1. Take a piece of paper and write down a line from the lyrics of all (or some) of the songs you put in your playlist, leaving one word missing.
2. Your partner must guess and write down the missing word, for example:

*"Jingle bells, jingle bells, jingle all the **(way)**" "We wish you a **(Merry Christmas)**"*

Start the songs and let the game begin!!
Besides guessing the missing words, you can play to guess the title and the artist.

REMEMBER... YOUR TASK IS TO GO OVER ALL THE SONGS IN YOUR PLAYLIST TO GET INTO THE RHYTHM OF CHRISTMAS... WHICH IS ALMOST HERE!

♥ 5

CINNAMON COOKIES

Today, you're chefs (or almost...)

Solve a series of clues to discover the necessary ingredients to prepare tonight's dessert:

CINNAMON CHRISTMAS COOKIES, STAR-SHAPED SHORTBREAD

CLUE 1
"I am the basic ingredient for almost all desserts, white and light; without me, there is no substance. Who am I?"

CLUE 2
"I melt in the heat, making everything softer and tastier. I am an ally to every crumbly dessert."

CLUE 3

"Sweet like Christmas memories, I melt in the heat and make the flavor of every little cookie shine."

CLUE 4

"I am enclosed in a shell, I have the power to bind everything together. Without me, the dough would never hold up."

CLUE 5

"I am invisible until I spring into action. I lift every dough and make your dessert rise, even if you don't see me."

CLUE 6

"I am the spice that tastes like Christmas. Warm, fragrant, and enveloping, I immediately make you think of winter."

CLUE 7

"I'm not sweet, but without me, even desserts lose their flavor. I find the right balance in every dish."

CLUE 8

"I am a light powder that settles like snow on the dessert, giving it an enchanting and vanilla-scented final touch."

HAVE YOU DISCOVERED ALL THE INGREDIENTS?

Go to the solutions page to find all the ingredients you need to prepare your cookies.

THEN

DURING THE DAY
BUY THE INGREDIENTS YOU ARE
MISSING...

WHAT ELSE YOU'LL NEED...

- 1 Oven or 1 Air Fryer
- 1 Baking Sheet
- 1 Star-shaped cookie cutter (otherwise, you can do it by hand with a knife)
- 1 Food wrap
- 1 Parchment paper
- 1 Rolling pin

Great, do you have everything?

YOU'LL FIND THE RECIPE ON THE
NEXT PAGE

INGREDIENTS

- 200 g flour
- 80 g Butter
- 4 tablespoons Sugar
- 2 Eggs
- Half a packet of baking powder for desserts
- 1 teaspoon Ground cinnamon
- 1 pinch Salt
- Vanilla icing sugar (for decorating)

PREPARATION
For the Cinnamon Shortbread:

Sift the flour into a bowl, add the other dry ingredients: sugar, cinnamon, salt, baking powder, and mix. Cut the butter into pieces and incorporate it into the flour, pinching the mixture until you get crumbs. Finally, add the eggs one at a time and quickly knead the dough, even transferring it to a counter. Wrap the shortbread dough in plastic wrap and place it in the refrigerator to cool.

BAKING THE COOKIES

Preheat the oven to 350F (about 180C). Using a lightly floured rolling pin, flatten the dough onto a sheet of parchment paper to about 1/4 inch (half a centimeter) thickness. This way, you won't need to add more flour. Use a cookie cutter to cut the dough into star shapes.

Transfer the cookies to two baking sheets lined with parchment paper and bake for about twenty minutes. Check on them during the last 5 minutes, moving the baking sheet if necessary.

Remove from the oven and transfer the cookies to a wire rack so they can cool. Alternatively, you can flip them over on the baking sheet itself to prevent steam from forming underneath the cookie.

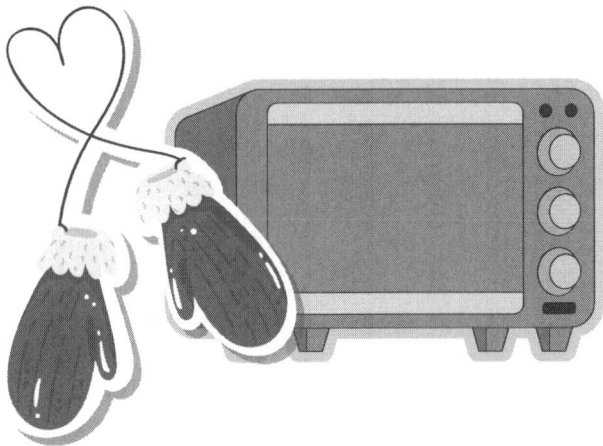

MAZE ESCAPE

HELP SANTA CLAUS REACH THE TREE

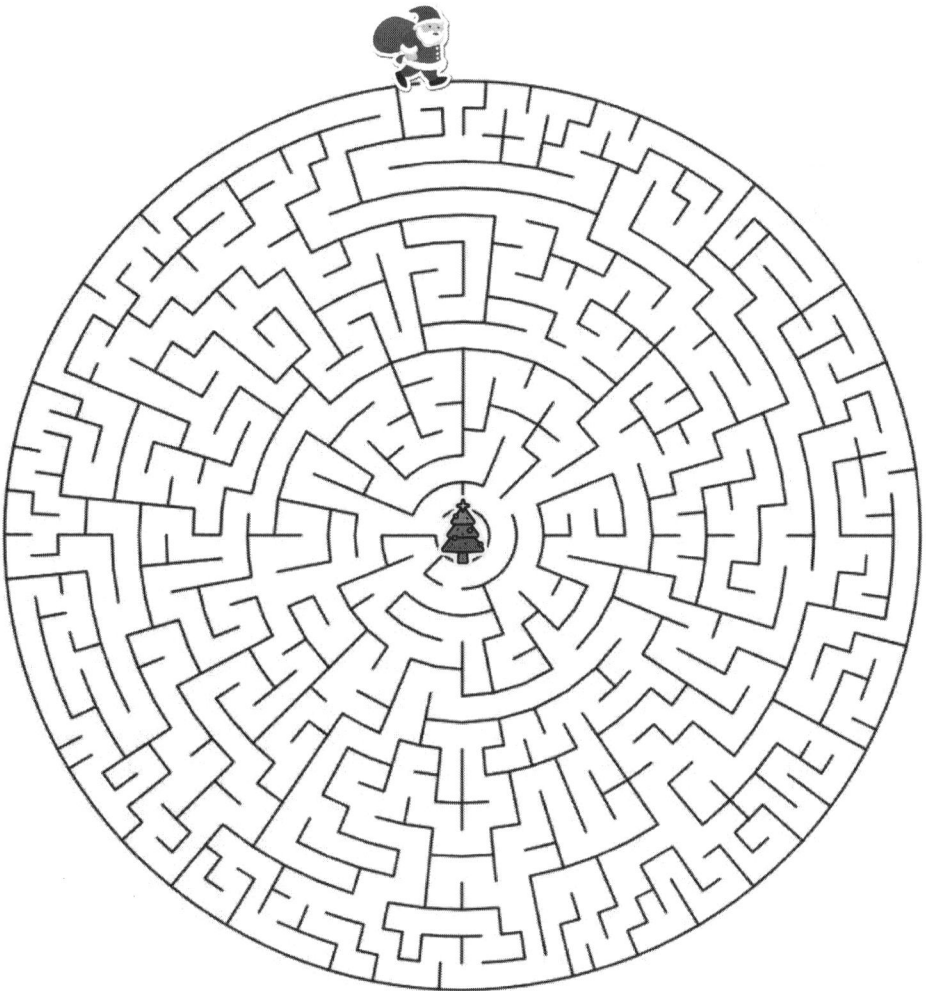

❤7

THE SCENTS OF CHRISTMAS

Take turns guessing the holiday scents.

You'll need to guess some Christmas-related scents using only your sense of smell!

WHAT TO PREPARE DURING THE DAY

BOTH OF YOU, DURING THE DAY, MUST FIND AT HOME, OR BUY, SCENTS THAT REMIND YOU OF CHRISTMAS.

GATHER THEM IN A BAG SO YOUR PARTNER CAN'T SEE WHAT THEY ARE.

Some examples:

Typical Christmas spices and aromas (cinnamon, cloves, orange, vanilla, etc.)

READY TO PLAY?

INSTRUCTIONS:

1. Take turns blindfolding yourselves.
2. Place the various aromas in containers / small plates / bowls.
3. The blindfolded partner must try to guess the scent only by smelling it.
4. For each correct scent, you'll earn a point.
5. In the end, the winner can choose a Christmas wish that the other partner must fulfill.

WHO GUESSED THE MOST SCENTS?

Winner, write your Christmas wish here:

LET'S DECORATE THE TREE

The time has finally come to dust off the Christmas tree and ornament boxes and put up the tree... the house is taking on a festive look!!

But... this year you'll do it differently: the first part of the tree decorations will be earned by **solving a quiz or a riddle**.
Each partner must answer **4 questions**, and only after completing each challenge will it be possible to add a new decoration to the tree.

ARE YOU READY TO TURN DECORATING THE TREE INTO A CHRISTMAS ADVENTURE?

QUESTIONS FOR THE FIRST PARTNER:

1
What is the color of Christmas that traditionally represents purity?

They are red and sweet, often found in bags during the holidays. They are traditional in Christmas baskets, but you don't eat them right away... What are they?
2

3
In which Italian city is the tradition of setting up a huge living Nativity scene that attracts tourists from all over the world famous?

On what date does Saint Nicholas Day fall, a historical figure who inspired the character of Santa Claus?
4

QUESTIONS FOR THE SECOND PARTNER:

1 Which Christmas plant is known for bringing good luck and is hung above the door for kissing underneath?

2 In which country was the tradition of the decorated Christmas tree born?

3 It has no legs or arms, but at the end of December, it gets everyone dancing. Sometimes it's gold, sometimes silver, and it's found on holiday tables... What is it?

4 In which Nordic country is the real Santa Claus said to live, according to modern tradition?

THE WISH BOX

Share your wishes for Christmas.

Today you must create a **"wish box"** and insert notes with clues that lead to each wish.

MATERIALS NEEDED

- A box
- 3-4 notes for each partner
- Pens or markers

INSTRUCTIONS:

- Each partner writes 3-4 Christmas wishes and places the notes in the wish box.
- The same day or in the following days, you can read each wish and discuss it together.

You can also organize a mini scavenger hunt at home and insert the notes into the box to later draw one... and the extracted wish must be granted, in turn

THE RESOLUTIONS LIST

Write your New Year's resolutions together.

Today, you will build a list of resolutions for the new year together, but you'll have to **earn each resolution** by solving questions and completing small challenges.
Each riddle solved will help you formulate a new resolution for your relationship and for yourselves.

MATERIALS NEEDED

- A sheet of paper to write the list or a notebook.
- Pen

INSTRUCTIONS:

- Solve each question or challenge together. When you answer correctly or complete a challenge, write the related resolution on the list.
- By the end, you will have a list of **10 resolutions** to improve your relationship and your life in the new year.

LET'S BEGIN...

QUESTION

What is one skill you would like to improve in each other to strengthen your bond?

CHALLENGE

Take 2 minutes of silence to reflect on one personal aspect to work on, and then share it with each other.

What is one thing you would like to do together more often, but never find the time to do?

QUESTION

CHALLENGE

Take a calendar and set a date for a special couple's activity that you will do in the new year.

What is one positive habit that each of you could bring into the relationship to improve daily life?

CHALLENGE

Choose a book to read together or a new hobby to start in the new year.

ARE YOU WRITING EVERYTHING DOWN?

What compromise could you both make to reduce unnecessary arguments?

QUESTION

CHALLENGE

Write a list together of 3 things you've always wanted to do but have put off.

What is a quality in your partner that you appreciate the most and would like to see grow?

LAST CHALLENGE...

Create a small daily ritual that will bring you closer (for example, a kiss every morning before starting the day or a sweet message during the day).

THE RESOLUTIONS LIST IS ONLY THE FIRST STEP.

THE REAL GOAL IS TO COMMIT TOGETHER TO ACHIEVE THEM, TURNING IDEAS INTO ACTIONS, STRENGTHENING YOUR RELATIONSHIP EVERY DAY.

♥ 11

SURPRISE DINNER

Organize a surprise dinner for your partner.

One partner will choose a restaurant for dinner, but must keep the location secret until the very last moment. The other partner will have to guess the restaurant using clues.

WHAT TO DO FIRST

Choose which of the two partners will select the restaurant.

Done ?

Write the organizer's name here:

WHAT TO DO NOW...

THE ORGANIZER MUST NOW:

1. Choose and book the restaurant.
2. Prepare clues to send to their partner throughout the day.

Clue Examples:
1. "There's a dish we both love here, and it's the best in the city."
2. "It's a place we went to once, and we ate a very good dessert."
3. "Their specialty has something to do with the sea.

The organizer's goal is to have their partner guess the name of the restaurant by 6:30 PM... otherwise, dinner is canceled!

DID THEY GUESS IT?

☐ yes   ☐ no

Enjoy your dinner!

FIND THE HIDDEN OBJECTS

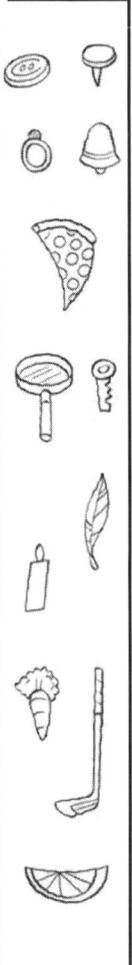

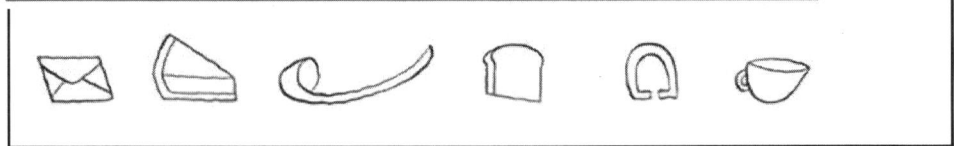

CHRISTMAS LIGHTS

Decorate one room of the house with Christmas lights.

Today you will add a festive touch to a room in your house...
BUT ONLY AFTER SOLVING A SERIES OF CHRISTMAS-THEMED QUESTIONS.

Example of a room to decorate: the entryway, the bathroom, the bedroom...

Take turns answering the questions and decorating the room; the one who guesses puts up the decoration!

IMPORTANT:
During the day, if you don't have them, buy some decorations, like Christmas lights, to bring the festive touch to the chosen room!

LET'S START WITH THE QUESTIONS

1 What is the city famous for its Christmas lights display called "Dyker Heights Christmas Lights"?

2 Which country is considered the birthplace of the tradition of decorating the Christmas tree with lights?

3 In which year was the first electric illumination of a Christmas tree switched on?

A. 1865 – B. 1882 – C. 1912 – D. 1935

4 Which Italian city is famous for its spectacular Christmas illumination in the "Via di San Gregorio Armeno"?

In which city is the famous "Christmas Market" located, one of the oldest and most famous in Europe?

5

6

What famous Christmas song begins with the words "You better watch out, you better not cry..."?

HAVE YOU GUESSED THE ANSWERS?

How did your Christmas room turn out?

TAKE A SOUVENIR PHOTO OF YOUR CHRISTMAS ROOM AND PASTE IT HERE:

NIGHT OUT

Plan a fun night out with hidden clues...

Who organized the dinner out?
Great... now the roles are reversed!

HERE'S HOW IT WORKS:

The planning partner must organize a fun night out (movies, bowling, an exhibition or event),
but they must provide clues to get the other partner to guess the activity before you leave.

INSTRUCTIONS

Write 3 clues for the evening and have your partner solve them.
Give them the necessary clues until they guess it, and start the evening!

MEMORY HUNT

A scavenger hunt for special memories from the last year (or your relationship in general).

Create a home scavenger hunt, hiding objects or notes related to important moments in your relationship. Each object will lead to a special memory.

INSTRUCTIONS:

Hide 5 significant objects or photos around the house, each with a clue that will lead to the next object. Each object represents a happy memory that you must tell out loud once it is found.

Clue Examples:
- *"Our first date at the cinema: look under something soft and cozy."*
- *"Remember when we went to the mountains? Go where we keep the travel gear."*

THE FLAVORS OF DECEMBER

Guess the Christmas flavors...

The perfect game to play after dinner.

INSTRUCTIONS

The couple must taste various typical Christmas foods or drinks such as panettone, gingerbread cookies, vin brulé (mulled wine), torrone (nougat), etc.

Materials needed:

At least 4-5 different Christmas foods/drinks (or prepared beforehand).

CHALLENGE

The one who guesses the most ingredients wins a prize that you must decide on before starting to play...

THE CHRISTMAS MOVIE QUIZ

Test your knowledge of Christmas movies with a fun quiz.

INSTRUCTIONS:

Take turns reading a question. The one who guesses the most movies chooses the movie to watch.

LET'S START

1 | Which Christmas movie tells the story of a child who defends himself alone from burglars at home?

In which movie is a selfish businessman visited by three ghosts on Christmas Eve who help him change his life?

2

Which movie follows the life of a young girl who, on Christmas Eve, falls asleep and is transported to an enchanted world, where she meets the Mouse King?

3

Which movie tells the story of a little girl who convinces a lawyer to defend a man who claims to be the real Santa Claus?

4

In which movie does a man switch bodies with Santa Claus and discovers how difficult it is to be the man in red on Christmas night?

5

Which movie tells the story of an enterprising elf who tries to save Christmas when Santa Claus mysteriously disappears?

6

In which movie does a rich and grumpy man discover the value of generosity after participating in a charity race to save an animal shelter at Christmas?

7

Which movie follows a child who receives a ticket for a special journey on a train headed to the North Pole on Christmas Eve?

8

Which movie follows a cynical town resident who hates Christmas and tries to ruin the festivities by stealing all the gifts, only to discover the true meaning of Christmas in the end?

9

Which movie follows the story of a girl **10**
who inherits an inn and discovers love and
the spirit of Christmas while trying to
restore it?

Who guessed the most titles?

Write the movie you want to
watch here:

PREPARE THE POPCORN...
ENJOY THE MOVIE!

FIND THE HIDDEN WORDS

Find the 14 Christmas-related hidden words.

```
A  P  A  N  E  T  T  O  N  E  L  S  O  T  C
T  E  S  A  S  L  E  G  N  A  F  O  E  U  R
N  D  L  A  C  F  B  I  G  S  A  M  D  P  E
A  T  L  I  N  R  O  I  E  T  O  M  L  N  F
T  I  E  S  A  T  F  O  R  C  L  N  U  E  T
I  O  D  A  K  T  A  E  B  Y  N  G  T  M  I
V  B  A  M  S  M  E  C  C  E  S  E  I  O  I
I  N  T  T  C  D  F  S  L  L  L  S  E  S  A
T  R  D  S  N  G  V  I  E  A  T  L  E  H  I
Y  L  F  I  N  E  S  I  R  L  U  V  S  A  P
R  T  E  R  E  O  G  L  E  T  L  S  G  I  H
P  R  C  H  E  H  L  T  D  E  R  S  I  T  N
E  R  S  C  D  P  O  N  G  I  S  E  H  P  O
M  L  E  Y  I  E  U  F  L  O  C  S  E  D  T
U  O  A  K  C  E  L  D  N  A  C  I  B  S  U
```

FIR TREE, ANGELS, SANTA CLAUS, BELLS, CANDLE, COMET, ELVES, CHRISTMAS, PANETTONE, NATIVITY, GIFTS, REINDEER, SLEIGH, MISTLETOE

GREETING CARD

Create a greeting card in 10 minutes that contains hidden clues about the gift your partner will receive for Christmas.

Each partner must create a special greeting card to give to their partner on Christmas Day. Using paper, pens, and decorations, each person must write a dedication, but the card won't be a simple wish: it will be a **mini escape game that contains hidden clues** about the gift they plan to give the other person.

UNLEASH YOUR IMAGINATION AND CREATIVITY!

CHALLENGE

In addition to including a sincere and affectionate wish, each partner must:

Insert **3 hidden clues** in the text that offer small suggestions about what the gift will be. The clues should not reveal too much, but allow the partner to get closer to the gift.

ADDITIONAL RULES:

- Do not reveal the content of the card before Christmas Day.
- Each partner must try to make the clues subtle, yet meaningful.
- The fun will be in seeing how close your partner gets to the gift just from the clues hidden in the card!

20

HIDDEN CHRISTMAS OBJECTS

A little relaxation amidst the Christmas preparations.

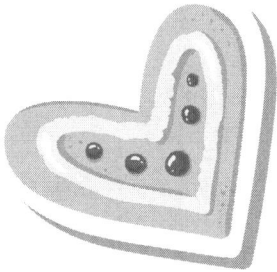

Since we are getting closer to Christmas and the to-do list seems endless, today you deserve a little break!

Today's challenge is to figure out together how many Christmas objects are hidden in this image.

Find all the hidden objects to be able to move on to tomorrow's game.

one   ——————————————

two   ——————————————

three   ——————————————

four   ——————————————

five   ——————————————

six   ——————————————

seven   ——————————————

eight   ——————————————

nine   ——————————————

ten   ——————————————

RIDDLES TO SOLVE AS A COUPLE

Have fun solving riddles together and write the answers below...

READY?
Let's begin...

What is that thing that the more there is, the less you see?

I am full of holes, but I always hold water. Who am I?

It has no legs, but it runs. It has no voice, but it speaks. What is it?

I am in everything and I am in nothing. What am I?

What can travel all over the world while staying in a corner?

It is so delicate that if you speak, you break it. What is it?

It can fill a room without taking up any space. What is it?

It gets undressed, but only when it's cold...

You open the door first and then enter, it enters first and then opens the door...

DID YOU GUESS THEM ALL?
Now, the one who guessed the most answers gets to give the other a task.
Be kind... it's Christmas, and you know... everyone is kinder at Christmas!

22

CAN YOU DECIPHER THE MOVIE?

1. _____

2. _____

3. _____

4. _____

5. _____

6. _____

7. _____

8. _____

9. _____

10. _____

DECIPHERED?

WHAT TO DO NOW:

- Take small paper notes; on each note, write the movie title.
- There should be 10 notes in total...
- Now put them in a bag and choose who picks the movie.

WHAT DID YOU GET?

Well... all that's left is to find the movie and spend an evening totally relaxing, rewatching a great movie from the past!

ENJOY THE SHOW!

23

THE MEMORY ALBUM FOR THE COMING YEAR

Create a memory album for the new year, designing the pages and deciding which moments to immortalize.

Work together to design an album where, in the coming year, you can paste photos and note the most beautiful moments spent together... *memories of trips, birthdays, special nights, etc.*

Using the clues, build an album divided by months, adding a page for each holiday or significant event, like a birthday, a trip (if you already have something planned)...

Of course, as the year goes on, you can modify and add events, activities, and special moments to the album.

WHAT TO LOOK FOR DURING THE DAY

- A blank notebook or cardstock pages to create the album
- Markers, glue, and various decorations (ribbons, stickers, glitter)

READY?
Let's begin...

1 The beginning is always cold and white, but it brings new resolutions. The month that opens the year should be decorated with snow and dreams yet to be realized. What is the month?

2 If 52 weeks form the perfect circle, divide them by four and you'll find the seasons. But don't forget that each season is made up of an equal number of parts. How many are these parts in the circle of the year?

3 A holiday arrives in spring, but its date is never fixed. It is celebrated after the first full moon following the equinox, and it brings with it a symbol of rebirth. What is this celebration?

It is the day each year the sun returns to its original position relative to your birth. A day that marks another lap around the sun, celebrated with candles and wishes. What is it?

4

GOOD JOB!
Have you uncovered the 4 clues?

Continue preparing your Memory Album... in the meantime, congratulations because tomorrow you can move on to the last activity!

HAPPY CHRISTMAS EVE

Today is a special day, we've finally reached Christmas! A quick escape game...

FIND THE 8 DIFFERENCES

SOLUTIONS

1 THE MOST BEAUTIFUL GIFT WE CAN RECEIVE AND GIVE IS THE TIME AND LOVE WE SHARE. OUR BOND IS THE REAL GIFT.

Did you discover the message?

☐ Yes   ☐ We got close   ☐ Far off

3 IN THE COLD OF WINTER, THE WARMTH OF THE LIGHTS REMINDS US THAT CHRISTMAS IS ALWAYS CLOSER.

Did you decipher the code?

☐ Yes   ☐ Obviously!

5 INGREDIENTS FOR THE COOKIES

- Clue 1: Flour - 7 oz (200 g) Type 1 flour
- Clue 2: Butter - 2.8 oz (80 g) Butter
- Clue 3: Sugar - 4 tablespoons Sugar
- Clue 4: Eggs - 2 Eggs
- Clue 5: Baking powder - Half a packet of baking powder for desserts
- Clue 6: Cinnamon - 1 teaspoon Ground cinnamon
- Clue 7: Salt - 1 pinch Salt
- Clue 8: Vanilla icing sugar - Vanilla icing sugar (for decorating)

6

8 QUESTIONS FOR THE FIRST PARTNER

- Answer Question 1 - White
- Answer Question 2 - Oranges
- Answer Question 3 - Greccio
- Answer Question 4 - December 6th.

QUESTIONS FOR THE SECOND PARTNER

- Answer Question 1 - Mistletoe
- Answer Question 2 – Germany
- Answer Question 3 - The Cotechino (A large Italian sausage)
- Answer Question 4 - Finland, specifically in Rovaniemi, in the Lapland region.

12

13

- Answer Question 1 - Brooklyn, New York.
- Answer Question 2 - Germany
- Answer Question 3 - 1882
- Answer Question 4 - Naples
- Answer Question 5 - Strasbourg, France
- Answer Question 6 - Santa Claus Is Coming to Town.

17

- Answer Question 1 - Home Alone
- Answer Question 2 - A Christmas Carol
- Answer Question 3 - The Nutcracker and the Four Realms
- Answer Question 4 - Miracle on 34th Street
- Answer Question 5 - The Santa Clause
- Answer Question 6 - Noelle
- Answer Question 7 - A Christmas Prince
- Answer Question 8 - Polar Express
- Answer Question 9 - The Grinch
- Answer Question 10 - Christmas Inheritance

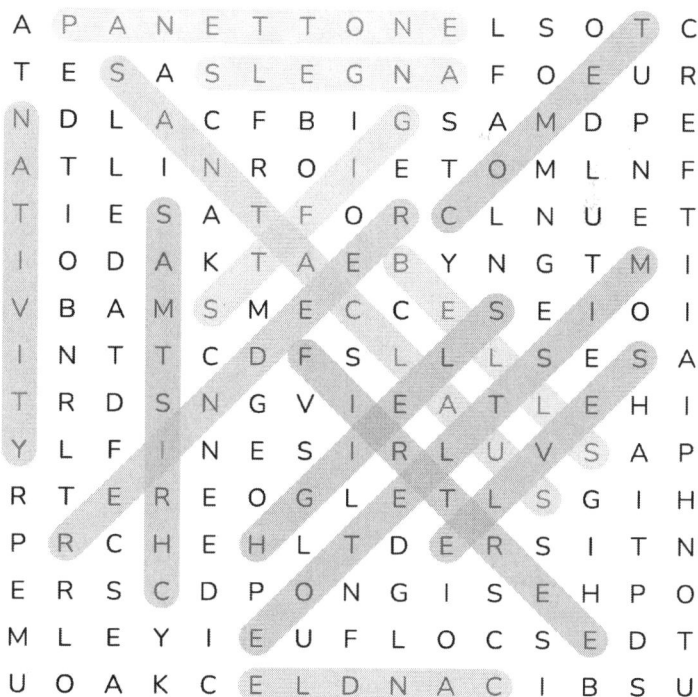

18

```
A  P  A  N  E  T  T  O  N  E  L  S  O  T  C
T  E  S  A  S  L  E  G  N  A  F  O  E  U  R
N  D  L  A  C  F  B  I  G  S  A  M  D  P  E
A  T  L  I  N  R  O  I  E  T  O  M  L  N  F
T  I  E  S  A  T  F  O  R  C  L  N  U  E  T
I  O  D  A  K  T  A  E  B  Y  N  G  T  M  I
V  B  A  M  S  M  E  C  C  E  S  E  I  O  I
I  N  T  T  C  D  F  S  L  L  L  S  E  S  A
T  R  D  S  N  G  V  I  E  A  T  L  E  H  I
Y  L  F  I  N  E  S  I  R  L  U  V  S  A  P
R  T  E  R  E  O  G  L  E  T  L  S  G  I  H
P  R  C  H  E  H  L  T  D  E  R  S  I  T  N
E  R  S  C  D  P  O  N  G  I  S  E  H  P  O
M  L  E  Y  I  E  U  F  L  O  C  S  E  D  T
U  O  A  K  C  E  L  D  N  A  C  I  B  S  U
```

20

one	Santa Claus
two	Reindeer
three	Snowmen
four	Gift Packages
five	Christmas Trees
six	Candelabras
seven	Snowflakes
eight	Small Books
nine	Baubles
ten	Stars

21

- The darkness
- The sponge
- The river
- The letter T (This is likely the answer to the "in everything and nothing" riddle)
- The stamp
- Silence
- A promise (This is likely the answer to the "fills a room" riddle based on the layout)
- The tree
- The key

1. Breakfast at Tiffany's

2. Edward Scissorhands

3. Mary Poppins

4. Aladdin

5. Memoirs of a Geisha

6. Brokeback Mountain

7. Finding Nemo

8. E.T.

9. Ghostbusters

10. The Devil Wears Prada

1. January

The album starts with a page for January, where you can note your resolutions for the new year and paste the first photos of the year.

2. 12 Months

The album must be divided by months, so it must have 12 sections, one per month. Leave about 10 pages for each month.

3. Easter

Add a page dedicated to Easter memories... when is it this year?

4. Birthday

Your birthdays cannot be missed... and they deserve a dedicated page.

Printed in Dunstable, United Kingdom